How To Study

Seventh Edition

THOMAS F. STATON, Ph.D.

Distributor:

HOW TO STUDY, P. O. Box 40273, Nashville, TN 37204

Seventh Edition

Copyright, 1982, by Emma D. Staton

Printed in the United States of America

Contents

PREFACE

TO THE STUDENT:

The ability to study and learn effectively and efficiently is a complex skill. To develop this skill requires both understanding of the principles of effective study and disciplined practice in applying them, just as building a garage requires both an understanding of the principles of carpentry and skill developed through practice in measuring, sawing, and hammering.

You would not expect to be able to deliver a hard, accurate tennis service your first time on the court simply because you had read in a book how to do it. Much practice would be required. Studying to learn most efficiently also requires conscientious practice.

This book will show you effective methods of studying, and it can guide you in establishing good study habits. No book, however, can enable you to learn faster and better if you do not practice the principles of efficient study. *Reading* this book is not enough. You must devote time and effort to applying in your study the principles it presents.

Remember this, too. The end result of practicing these principles and going through the PQRST steps described in this book is not simply efficient *studying*. The end result is *learning,* and being able to put to use what you have learned, whether it be to appreciate good literature, analyze an unknown chemical compound, or care for a patient in a hospital bed.

THOMAS F. STATON

April, 1982

Chapter 1

HOW LEARNING TAKES PLACE—INFORMATION PROCESSING

Chapter Outline

We see and hear millions of things we never notice.

This is sensory intake without memory or learning, and accounts for much poor "study."

By *noticing* something, you can put it into your short-term memory.

Short-term memory has limited capacity and use.

In studying, aim for long-term learning.

This requires *organizing* what you study and *comprehending* the meaning, significance, and implications.

This is *information processing*.

Effective learning involves two processes: *intake* and *memory*. Intake is, quite literally, the process of "taking in" what is to be learned. Seeing, reading, hearing, listening, and doing are the forms of intake most widely used by students, although people also "take in" impressions by touching, tasting, and smelling. Taking in information (called "sensory intake" or "sensory input" by psychologists) is seldom a problem for a college student, except one handicapped in one or more of his senses—a deaf or blind person, for instance.

The memory portion of learning (psychologists call this "retention") is a different matter. It may or may not take place when one of our senses takes in a particular bit of information. You probably have had the experience of reading a page in a textbook and, although your eyes had faithfully "read" every word (that is, there was sensory intake of every word), when you finished you did not remember a thing you had read. The key to effective study is learning how to remember what your eyes take in from a textbook and what your ears take in from a lecture or class discussion. This book will show you how you can "learn to remember" better. Keep in mind the difference between *sensory intake* and *memory.*

Sensory Intake

Have you ever looked at your watch to see what time it was, but when someone immediately asked you the time you were unable to remember? That, like reading a page and not remembering what you read, is an example of sensory intake that never reached even the lowest level of memory—the lowest level of learning.

Think of the literally millions of things you see and hear every day and, although you *see* or *hear* them, you do not *notice* them at all. You look at a tree and see thousands of leaves, you walk down a crowded sidewalk and see dozens of faces or through a store and see thousands of objects, or you stand beside a busy street and hear hundreds of different sounds—and never *notice* them. You can think of all these sights and sounds as being a "sensory parade." You *must* let them—or nearly all of them—go by without noticing them. If you tried to remember every object or every sound your senses took in . . . the very idea is ridiculous! You would be all day getting past the first house, with its thousands of bricks. You never would get anything worthwhile done.

There is a continual bombardment of our senses by thousands of things. So, in self-defense, we learn to be selective in what we notice—maybe a few faces in the crowd, perhaps one sound out of the many. The remainder of the sensory parade flows by us without ever really becoming a part of us in much the same way the money a check-out clerk in a supermarket handles flows by her without ever becoming *hers,* even though she holds it in her hand for a moment and counts it.

It is no wonder that frequently we let this necessary habit of not noticing *everything* carry over into our reading of a textbook. We let the words flow by without registering them, just as we let the faces, bricks, and trees flow by without noticing them. The crucial questions for students are: *How can we react more effectively to our sensory intake when we read something important, that we are supposed to be learning? How can we be sure to notice and to draw into our memory material we need to learn and remember?* We will work out the answers to these questions as we explore further into how memory and learning take place.

Most of this book is about memory and learning—how to learn more effectively, how to remember what you learn. Actually, memory and learning are closely related to each other, and the terms are used almost interchangeably throughout the book. It will help you in learning to study more effectively, however, to differentiate between *short-term* memory and *long-term* memory.

"Forgets" Where He Puts His Pencil? Don't Be Silly! Most of the Things We Say We "Forget" We Never Noticed, and Didn't Try to Remember.

Short-Term Memory

Short-term memory is the most shallow, the least permanent form of anything we remember or learn at all. Carrying a step further the analogy of the clerk handling countless coins and bills at the check-out counter, short-term memory is somewhat like the pay she receives, puts into her purse for a few hours, then quickly spends. It actually becomes hers, but only for a short time. In memory, this might correspond to your looking up a telephone number in the directory, remembering it long enough to dial, and then immediately forgetting it. Haven't you done that? Or picked up the name of a person at a large party or in a class but completely forgotten it within a few hours or days? Or crammed for an examination and forgotten most of it as you walked out the door of the examination room?

Just as our protective device of not noticing most of the sensory parade has a worthwhile use, so has short-term memory. Why clutter your mind forever with telephone numbers you never will call again, with names of people you may never see again, with facts of no concern or interest to you? You don't. You use your short-term memory to keep such facts until they have served their purpose, and then you forget them ... at least most of us do for most things not important to us.

Remembering something for a short time is not very hard to do. By conscious effort we can pull things—facts, ideas, impressions—out of the sensory parade and put them in our short-term memory, making them *ours*. We notice them and deliberately register them in our minds as something to remember, at least for a short period of time. When you look at your watch you can say to yourself, "It is now 10:28," and a few minutes later you can reach into your memory and pull out the fact that when you last checked the time it was 10:28. Or, when you are studying a history assignment, you can tell yourself, "The Connecticut Compromise resolved a serious conflict between large and small states by providing that one legislative body would be constituted on the basis of population, while the other would give equal representation to each state regardless of the size of its population." By deliberately telling yourself to remember that fact, you *can* remember it. You can put it in your short-term memory, to be taken out and used when needed. It is handily placed in the forefront of your mind where it jumps into your consciousness when you need it.

This is how you "learn" by cramming. Unfortunately, the amount we can keep in our short-term memory is comparatively small. You may be able to tell yourself to remember one telephone number and do it. But how about twenty numbers? How about not just the Connecticut Compromise but several hundred other facts presented in your history textbook? To remember great masses of facts or ideas, especially for any considerable length of time, you must have a better system than short-term memory affords. Psychologists have found that short-term memory will not hold an unlimited amount. Furthermore, things placed in the short-term memory usually fade out fast—like the telephone number you learned for just long enough to dial it. You might say that your "short-term memory purse" is insecure and lets its contents lose out along the way.

Long-Term Memory

Humans also have a long-term memory, which you can think of as a "learning bank." Psychologists say this mental storehouse can keep learning committed to it permanently, and its capacity is virtually unlimited. Like a bank, it can accommodate almost any amount and can keep it as long as you want it kept. Long-term learning is not merely intensified memory of short-term learning, but actually a different form of learning. It is not merely trying harder and harder to remember more and more unrelated facts or ideas. Basically, long-term learning involves *organizing* your short-term memories into a meaningful body of information and thinking them through to the point of *comprehending* their meaning, significance, and implications. This is what psychologists often call *information processing*.

The problem for the student is, *How do you put the things you need to remember into your long-term learning depository, and how do you get them out when you need them?* Long-term remembering involves securely depositing learning. Since it may total hundreds of thousands of facts, ideas, and concepts, it may take some effort to locate in your mind the one you need at a given moment. Don't you recall instances when you knew perfectly well a name, the answer to a test question, or the name of a tune, but could not quickly recall it, "locate it," when you wanted to? Just as it takes more planning and effort to establish a bank account for your money and write checks to get it out than to drop it into your pocket and take it out, it also takes more planning and effort to convert sensory input into long-term learning so it can be retrieved when you want it than to achieve short-term memory of it. But you must become able to do this if you ever are to acquire a college education.

Most of the remainder of this book is devoted to showing you how to process the information you acquire through reading or listening. It shows you how to convert that information into long-term learning in a form that will enable you to locate, recall, or retrieve it whenever you need to do so. Study the flow chart on page 11. This is a diagram of how information is processed by the mind. Relate its stages, processes, and explanations to what you have read in this chapter. Refer to it again as you find its functions discussed in later chapters.

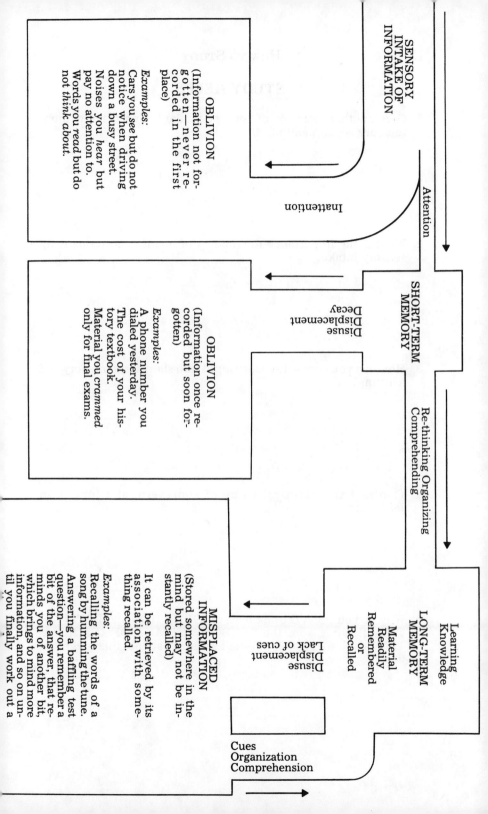

STUDY HELPS

1. Give another example of sensory intake taking place without memory accompanying it.

2. What is the importance to students of memory accompanying sensory intake?

3. How can you convert sensory input into short-term memory and learning?

4. Contrast the practical value of short-term and long-term learning.

5. Why do you think the channels of ATTENTION and INATTENTION flowing from the SENSORY INTAKE OF INFORMATION stage are of such different sizes? What does this suggest to you?

Chapter 2

HOW TO STUDY A READING ASSIGNMENT

Chapter Outline

Preview the assignment before reading it
Question what it may include
Read it, using your eyes and your brain
State in your own words what you have read
Test your memory of it a few hours or days later

Suppose you sit down in your easy chair and read a book that tells you how to swim. Then you go on about your business the next few days, and only think of it again when you get into the pool. Naturally, your stroke will have improved little, if any, as a result of your reading. Similarly, if you merely read this book, you will be largely wasting your time. In the first place, just reading it probably will get its ideas only into your short-term memory, never get them deposited into your long-term learning. In the second place, this book is not simply an informational bulletin. Rather it describes procedures that you must *practice*, if they are to be helpful to you. It presents a way to process information effectively, which can result in long-term learning. You will not be able to study appreci-

ably better by only *reading* this book, but if you *study* it, come to understand the principles and procedures it outlines, and *practice* using them when you study, you can learn more in the hours you spend studying.

Reading Isn't Enough—You Must Practice What You Read.

To learn well from this book requires efficient reading, but few people read as well as they can *learn* to read. So first of all we will present a method of studying reading assignments to get the greatest possible amount of long-term learning and memory from whatever amount of time you spend.

This method of study is called the PQRST method. It is easy to remember because, as you recognize, five consecutive letters of the alphabet are involved. It is a plan for studying that has been devised to take fullest advantage of the psychological factors which help people learn. It has been tested by having one group of students prepare their study assignments using the PQRST method, and another group use their usual study methods. Students using the PQRST method of study have consistently made higher average scores on tests over material studied than have the students who used their "natural" study methods. This type of experiment has been repeated in many different ways, and it has been found that the groups using the PQRST method tend to make better grades on the tests, whether all groups spend a short time or a long time studying. In other words, if you have only a short time available for studying, you probably will learn and remember more if you go through all of the PQRST steps, fast and briefly, rather than omitting any of the steps.

In each of the five steps that follow there are two things we need to notice especially:

(1) *How is the step accomplished?*

(2) *What good will result from doing this step well?*

The PQRST Method of Study

The first step in the PQRST method of study is a **Preview** of the material to be studied. You know what a preview is. Many times you have seen a preview of the coming attraction at the movies—a brief glance at what is coming later, to see its general plan and ideas, to interest you in seeing more, but not to get all the details. This is exactly what you should do in the **Preview** step of the PQRST method.

You can get this preview in several different ways. Many authors of textbooks break their material into *topics* or *sub-topics*. Some put brief descriptive headings at the beginning of these topics. If this is done, reading these headings will give you a general idea of what the subject is about. The cartoons beginning each step of the PQRST method of study in this chapter serve as topic headings.

At the beginning of each chapter of this book you will find a *Chapter Outline* which will give you a brief preview of what the chapter contains. Few authors provide this study help, but the table of contents of many textbooks contains a list of the topics discussed under each chapter title. Always look at the table of contents of any text you are about to study to see if it provides you with this sort of preview of chapters. Occasionally looking back to the topic headings listed under each chapter title in the table of contents as you study will help you keep the organization of the material clearly in mind, and this is quite important, as we will see later.

If the author does not use topic headings, you may find at the first or the last of paragraphs *key sentences* which give the general idea of the paragraph. A quick look will show you if the author has used this study aid. If he or she has, these key sentences will serve the same purpose topic headings would.

Perhaps, if he or she has not done any of these things, the writer has put a *summary* at the end of the chapter, including in that summary the main ideas presented. This gives you a fine way of previewing the material. Read this summary *first*, with the idea of getting from it the general picture of the chapter.

If none of these aids to previewing is present, you must depend on the most difficult but the most valuable and helpful of all the preview methods. This is *scanning*. Scanning consists of running your eyes rapidly down a page, not reading word by word or even looking at every sentence, but picking a phrase here and there to get an idea of what the author is writing about and the general approach he or she is taking. Developing the ability to scan rapidly and well requires some practice, but, once mastered, this ability is a valuable aid for thorough study and a great help in rapidly surveying material.

Performing the **Preview** step properly will give you the general picture the author is setting forth in his writing, and will let you begin to see the main ideas he is trying to put across. Seeing exactly what he is trying to do helps you look for and recognize the most important points as you read.

Previewing also lets you see the *organization* of the subject matter you are to study. It is like looking at a picture of a jigsaw puzzle before trying to put the pieces together. Seeing the whole picture of a chapter will help tremendously in understanding how each topic fits in with the other topics around it. This step in the study process shows the author's organization and helps you establish why you are to study this material. There is some reason to believe that getting a clear picture of the organization of material you are studying may be the biggest single key to long-term learning of that material. In the next chapter we will discuss more fully *organization* and its importance to long-term learning. At this point, just note that in *previewing* you should be looking for the over-all pattern—the "Big Picture"—of what the author is presenting.

In Previewing An Assignment, Get The Big, Over-all Picture.

I FIGURE OUT EXACTLY WHAT I SHOULD GET OUT OF IT

Question

The second step in the PQRST method of study is **Question.** While you are going through the **Preview** step, or even when you read the title of the chapter or topic, stop a minute and ask yourself, "Just what should be included in a topic with this title? As you go through the **Preview** step, make up some questions you think might be answered by a careful reading of the material.

Suppose, for example, you are to study an assignment on the life of Elizabeth Barrett Browning. Questions you might expect to find answered are: *What was her childhood like? How is this reflected in the things she wrote? What could account for her writing poems in such vein as "How Do I Love Thee?" and "Grief"? Was she influenced heavily by the writings of any other authors? How has her writing influenced other writers?* All these questions might be made up from the title of the assignment alone. You may be able to get more detailed questions while previewing the topic.

Often you will find a list of the author's questions at the end of a chapter. Look for such a list *before* you begin your detailed reading. (See the Study Helps at the end of chapters in this book, for example.) Read them over after your preview and keep them in mind while you carefully read the assignment. You will find that looking over this list of questions fits in naturally with reading the summary of the chapter before you read the chapter in detail, as both usually come at the end of the chapter.

You can see from this that one of the ways to improve study is to use to the fullest every possible help that the author of your textbook gives. This sometimes means, however, that you will not take things in the order in which he or she put them. If he or she put something (a summary, for instance, or a list of study questions) at the *end* of a chapter but it can help you more to read it *first*, by all means read it first!

What do you profit from this **Question** step? We already have mentioned that it is good to know exactly what to look for when you are studying. The more you are trying to find the answers to good, intelligent questions as you study, the more effective your learning is likely to be. These questions you find or formulate give *immediate* things to look for as you begin reading. The **Preview** step already has clued you in to the over-all idea of what you should get from studying the chapter. The questions you have in mind are pointers, telling you what you might look for in each sub-topic, sentence by sentence and paragraph by paragraph. They encourage you to watch for details in your reading. They help you pay closer attention to what you are reading, help you *concentrate* by giving you something to hunt for as you study.

Learning to formulate questions will help you, too, in preparing for examinations. High marks on examinations are not the only reason for study, but it would be ridiculous to pretend that they were unimportant in schoolwork. Only a limited number of good questions can be asked on a given body of subject material. As you become skillful in making up questions as you study, you will find more and more of the questions you compose also appearing on tests. As you become familiar with the particular testing habits of individual teachers, you can spot more and more of their test questions. Having especially studied even a few questions which appear on a test can be a great help! If you will write down the questions you make up as you do this **Question** step in your daily study and review them when preparing for a test, they may raise your test grades considerably.

Our third step in the PQRST method is **Read.** Effective reading calls for *reaction.* When we start to read a study assignment, many of us pull up an easy chair, lean back in it, prop up our feet on the desk and the book in our lap, and read with our eyes. Our eyes are active. They read, word for word, everything written on the page. But all too frequently our mind is relaxed. The result is that we read a paragraph, word for word, and then find that we have not the least idea what we have just read. Our intake of the material never went past being part of the "sensory parade" mentioned in Chapter 1.

The keynote to effective reading is *reaction*—that is, thinking hard about what you are reading. Your mind is not thirsty soil which soaks up knowledge without effort, just by coming into contact with it. Knowledge is more like a football which has been kicked into the air; you must pursue and catch it before you can put it to use.

The extent to which your mind is alert, considering each point as you read it and how each idea is relating to others to build up the over-all pattern or organization of the material, is the extent to which you are going to learn what you are reading. Learning is a job requiring your brain to be in action, and it takes place when you react energetically and aggressively to the material you are to learn. (Additional tips on promoting *reaction* in your study will be given in Chapter 4.)

The fourth step in our method of study is **State.** By this we mean, say over in your own words what you have read. When you finish reading a paragraph, look away from your book and state in your own words what the author has said. After you become proficient in the **State** step, you may find it preferable to read an entire section, or

even a chapter, before stopping to restate what you have read. If you read several pages before restating what you have read, it may help you to look at a topic heading and then in your mind recall what was in that topic.

If the book you are reading does not have topic headings, then try underlining while you read. The lining will recall to you the important points, and you should then think through them to reconstruct the topic as fully as possible in your own mind. If it is not your book, of course, you will not underscore in it. In this case, you might outline in your mind what you have read and then check with the book to see if your outline is an accurate one. After completing your outline, it is still a good idea to think over the points to see if you remember enough of the details to fill in the facts at which your outline hints.

Even better than underlining as a device to help you remember important ideas is making marginal notes of key ideas you encounter as you read. Studying with a pencil in your hand is a good habit to get into. In the margin beside each paragraph jot down a few key words that reflect the main ideas. Then, when you have read a topic or a chapter and are ready for the **State** part of your studying, glance at your marginal note beside a paragraph and proceed to elaborate on the idea it suggests. See how nearly you can recall and state in your own words the entire content of the paragraph. You will find that practice in making these pertinent marginal notes as you read and recalling a paragraph from them will develop your ability to recall the contents of a paragraph more completely than you now believe possible.

It is important that you do this recalling *verbally,* that

is, by actually speaking the words aloud or under your breath. Just thinking, "Oh . . . ummmmmmmmmmm . . . uh . . . I remember . . . that's about . . . yeah, I know all about that," isn't good enough! Each one of us has had the experience of thinking of an idea and saying to himself or herself, "Yeah, that's a good idea, I know all about it." But then when we started to explain the idea to someone else, we found ourselves unable to put it into words. An idea that is so hazy, so nebulous, that it cannot be explained in actual, specific words is not likely to be of much value to anyone. As you know very well, you can neither talk about a subject nor take a test on it to very good advantage if you have only a vague, muddy idea of what it is all about. And, after all, the only way we can tell whether we have a topic clearly enough in mind to put it into words is by trying to put it into words! So, do just exactly this.

In reconstructing the topic from your outline, underlining, topic headings, or marginal notes, put your ideas into actual words to be sure you have them clearly in mind. Say them to yourself or aloud. If you do this step thoroughly, it will force you to *react* in your studying, and this is absolutely necessary for learning. You are engaging in important mental activity when you accurately restate the topics in your own words. Doing this also makes certain that you understand the *organization* of the material. It is impossible to know a subject thoroughly just by knowing each individual fact relating to that subject, with only a faint idea of how these facts fit together to make up the whole. You can't tell the author's story in your own words unless you have clearly in mind the big picture, that is, the *organization* of what he or she is saying.

The **State** step in your study also does much to guarantee *comprehension*, which ranks in the class with *organization* as essential to putting what you learn into your long-term memory bank. To reconstruct a topic in your own words, you must have a knowledge of the main point and an understanding of the real meaning of the subject. You must see what the words and ideas are all about. If you know the organization the author follows, and if you can express his or her ideas in *your own words,* probably you have learned the material well enough to be able to put it to use. (On the other hand, an unthinking person may be able to repeat from mere rote memory, with great accuracy, a given set of facts and still have no comprehension of what they mean; a parrot may be able to do this, too!) You will profit from what you learn just to the extent that you can apply this knowledge to situations where you need it, whether they be final exams or other activities in life.

Performing this step will give you a valuable and reliable way of seeing how effective your study has been, whether or not you need to study more on a given topic, and on which spots additional study is most needed. It is a waste of time to re-study material you already know and understand thoroughly, or to go on to new material when supporting material already *covered* has not been *learned.* If you can re-create what you have read from your outline notes, you know it well enough to go on to something else without spending further time on it. If you cannot, proceeding to new material at this point is likely to add more vague, useless fragments of material to your store, consuming more of your time and achieving no usable results. The **State** step gives you an immediate check on whether, in actuality, you have lifted what you have read out of the "sensory intake" category into your memory.

As you learn to stretch your *stating* over several paragraphs—even several topics—instead of *stating* the content of each paragraph as you finish reading it, you are making surer that you are putting that material into your long-term learning bank, not just short-term. You might be able to remember what is in the paragraph you just finished reading without actually having much comprehension of its meaning or much grasp of the organization of the whole thing. But to go back and, merely by looking at your marginal notes, *state* the essentials of an entire section or chapter, you will need to have grasped the overall pattern and message of that section or chapter. If you do have this grasp, the chances are good that you have made that information you read a part of your long-term learning.

The importance of *stating* in your own words what you have studied can hardly be overemphasized. Actual laboratory experiments have shown that the person who has a given amount of time to study a topic, whether that amount of time be fifteen minutes or five hours, generally makes better scores on tests on that material if he spends *at least half of his total study time* in reflective thinking (that is, thinking over what he has read—as he must do in the **State** step). This means that if you have an hour to study a chapter, you generally will do better to spend thirty minutes, or a little less, in your **Preview** and **Read** steps and at least thirty minutes in your **Question** and **State** steps. A moment's thought will show you that the **Question** and the **State** steps involve practically the same type of mental processes. Both require you to think, to use your memory, and to organize or figure out ideas and information for yourself, through your own efforts. The **Preview** and **Read** steps, on the other hand, are similar in that both of them are concerned primarily with your trying to get the author's picture. So, remember, spending half of your time on the two steps requiring reflective thinking and only half of your study time in actual reading seems to be the best idea. Many experimenters recommend spending as much as two-thirds of your study time in reflective thinking, but *hardly a one of them recom-*

mends spending less than half.

It is very easy to slight this reflective thinking part of your job, because it is harder to think than it is to read. Furthermore, it is easier to kid yourself that you have thought through a topic when you really have not thought it through at all than it is to kid yourself that you have read the pages when you really have not. So the safest idea probably is to make yourself a rule that you will use your watch to guarantee that you are not shortchanging this step in your study process. *Give the* **State** *step plenty of work if you are really interested in learning and remembering!*

The final step in your PQRST technique of study is **Test.** Perhaps you assume that, schools and teachers being what they are, you can be assured of plenty of tests without devising any of your own! But **Test** in the PQRST system is one of the necessary checks you run on yourself to assure yourself better grades on those other tests inevitably to follow.

This step is really a shortened run-through of the **State** step, just described, but performed *some time after* your first study, for purposes of review. It is really a form of review. The thing to remember is that this review should consist in *reflective thinking* on the material being reviewed rather than in merely running your eyes over it. The same things that have been said about *reaction* and the **State** step apply here. Memory of material does not take place when you review simply because your eyes pass over it a second or third time, but as a result of what your brain does when it thinks a topic through for a second or third time.

An excellent way of carrying out this **Test** step of study is looking at the marginal notes you made during the **Read** step and reconstructing the material identified or summarized in these marginal notes, as in the **State** step. It is probably the most effective method of reviewing for a test.

If you think of review in terms of testing how much you remember and then repairing weaknesses, rather than merely running your eyes over notes or materials, you will find that you will remember more, and be able to use it to better advantage, in taking tests or putting it to any other use. So when you review, use a shortened version of the **State** step. We call this **Test.**

It is a good idea to test your memory of what the instructor said in class, too. As part of the **Test** step, look over the notes you took in class and try to reconstruct from them what the instructor said on the subject. Finally, check your class notes against the text. See if they agree or if you need to ask a question to get their relationship clear. Get what the instructor says and what the text says related in your mind into one organized body of facts and ideas.

This step, even more than the **State** step, also checks the extent to which you have converted what you have studied into long-term learning rather than merely having dropped it into your short-term memory bag.

In Testing Yourself On Today's Lesson, Tie Together What Your Text Says And What Your Instructor Said In Class.

This is the PQRST technique of study. Every step has been proved an important link in a chain that leads to most effective study. It can work no miracles. It cannot give learning without your spending time and effort. However, if you are thinking, "This system may be good, but it would take more time than I can spend studying, and it is too complicated to follow," remember these three things:

1. *Whatever amount of time you spend,* if you will divide it between reading and reflective thinking as described here, you will learn and remember more than if you leave out the reflective thinking part.

2. When scattered bits of time are spent in study without a regular study period, and when no systematic plan of study is followed, the amount of time spent will not give as good results as the same total amount of time would give if it were planned and used systematically, as in the PQRST method.

3. Most people report that when they actually try the PQRST method it proves to be much simpler and easier to put into effect than they thought it would be. So, give it a trial. Practice it a half-dozen times and you will find that it works very smoothly and simply. A little time spent in developing skill in using the PQRST method will pay big dividends in time saved in later study and in better grades made.

There is no substitute for time and work in learning. However, if you will regularly practice the procedures and principles set forth here, you will process the information your eyes and ears take in in such a manner that you will get more learning and memory from whatever amount of time and effort you put into your study. Try it!

STUDY HELPS

1. How does the **Preview** step help you learn?

2. What function does the **Question** step perform in aiding effective study?

3. What should you do to **Read** most effectively?

4. List the benefits to be derived through use of the **State** step.

5. How does the **Test** step differ from the way most students review?

THIS WON'T IMPROVE THE EFFECTIVENESS OF YOUR STUDY...

BUT THIS WILL!

Chapter 3

LISTENING TO A LECTURE

Chapter Outline

If only your ears are at work when you are "listening" to a lecture, you will learn practically nothing. Unless your mind is actively concentrating on what is being said, reacting to it, thinking about it, mulling it over, interpreting it, relating it to the things you already know, and filtering out the significance of facts and ideas as they are given to you, the time you spend in a lecture is largely wasted. On the other hand, probably the biggest time-saver in the whole area of studying is effectively listening to lectures and classroom discussions.

To get started properly, sit where you can hear the speaker. If you are assigned a seat where you cannot hear the teacher, tell him or her so. He or she will allow you to change your seat. Don't be bashful about making such a request. Professors want you to listen to what they say and hear it clearly. The typical professor will bring out in his or her lectures virtually everything in the course he or she believes is really important for you to learn. The student who hears, understands, and remembers what the instructor says is almost certain to do well on tests in the course.

Just as there are procedures that will increase the effectiveness of your study of a reading assignment, there are procedures which will increase the amount you will learn from a lecture.

Previewing the Lecture

As in studying a book, you can listen to a lecture most successfully and with greater comprehension if you have previewed what the lecturer likely will talk about. Certainly, this is not as easy to do as it is to preview a chapter in a textbook. At first thought you may say it is impossible to preview what somebody is going to say sometime in the future. But use your brain, your imagination, your creative thinking ability! From the study assignment you have been given you usually can deduce with fair accuracy what your professor will talk about in the next lecture. He or she ordinarily will talk along one of two lines, or a combination of them, and your own thoughtful study of the assignment will prepare you to obtain maximum benefit from either course followed. The teacher may (1) discuss the topics in the assignment itself, elaborating on what is said in the assigned text. In this case, your knowledge of what the text presents enables you to follow his or her lecture intelligently and with comprehension. He or she may (2) discuss topics related to the assignment but not covered in the text. Your clear comprehension of the textual material will enable you to perceive how the material he or she is presenting relates to the subject as a whole, and will give you a framework within which to organize and interpret those facts and ideas.

Listening Effectively

You should recognize that effective listening is a relatively high-level skill. Some of the procedures described here to improve the effectiveness of your listening are not simple things that you can do automatically. It will require practice on your part to develop skill in doing them, but faithful practice in following these guides to listening to a lecture will enable you to listen with a higher degree of effectiveness and get more from the lecture than you previously thought possible.

Think About What is Being Said. The first and foremost thing to remember is that effective listening is an active mental process of *thinking* about what you are hearing. It involves the mental reaction of reasoning, weighing, and analyzing what is being said, not merely opening your ears so the words can reach your mind. You must *process* with your mind the *information* your ears take in. Sitting comfortably at ease, putting yourself into a receptive frame of mind and letting the lecturer's words flow into your brain, does not constitute effective listening. You have to concentrate, think, and reason.

But do you have trouble making yourself concentrate? Does your mind insist on wandering away from the lecture? Here are some suggestions to help you concentrate. They will help you listen effectively to lectures and learn most from the hours you spend in the classroom.

*You Must Listen With Your Mind As Well As
Your Ears To Learn!*

Look at the Lecturer. Do not expect your mind to stay on the lecture when your eyes are wandering to the window, your doodling, or the pretty girl two rows over. It won't. It will follow your eyes. Keeping your eyes fixed on the lecturer does not guarantee that your mind will stay fixed on what he or she is saying, but letting them stray practically guarantees that your mind will concern itself with something—anything—besides the lecture. (Of course, it also is common courtesy at least to appear to give attention to the person speaking.)

One exception to the rule of looking at the lecturer concerns note-taking. Obviously, you cannot take notes effectively without looking at the paper you are writing on. Most speakers feel that taking notes is the most sincere form of flattery, and they are delighted to see members of their class or audience busily recording their words and ideas.

Look for the General Plan, the Theme, of the Lecture. This is a crucial step in processing the information presented in the lecture. As an analogy, consider that the professor is building a house in this course. It is helpful for you to see the sketch of what the whole thing is to look like when it is finished. He or she has the blueprint, but you have a similar one in the contents of your textbook. So you have before you the possibility of seeing what the whole course is supposed to be when it is finished.

In every lecture the professor is building some specific part of this structure, the course, just as you are doing when you read a chapter in your text. Everything you are studying is contributing to the completion of a total structure. It also is contributing to the building of some specific part right now, so every day you need to see both what you are working on currently and its relation to the whole structure of the course. Otherwise, if you just start adding this to that, without knowing what you are building, you are much less likely to end up with a complete, well-integrated knowledge of the subject.

Listen for Ideas, Implications, and Significance—Not Merely Words and Facts. As the lecturer talks, constantly ask yourself, "What is she getting at? What does all this mean? What is the implication of what she is saying? How does this fit together with that? What does it all add up to?"

Your experience in reading paragraphs for meaning and implications, as described in Chapter 2, will prove highly valuable practice in enabling you to listen with analytical discrimination. As you learn to cut quickly and incisively to the meaning and significance of a paragraph you read, you also will find that you can listen to a lecture with much greater perception of the real meaning and implications of what you hear than you could in the past.

Naturally, it is necessary for you to learn and remember a large number of facts in your studying and listening, but good scholarship and the desire for knowledge require that you go far beyond mere memory of facts. They demand that you sift and rearrange those facts in your mind to form a meaningful concept of the subject. You cannot do all this without the intense mental activity that is a prerequisite for effective listening—mental activity that involves analysis, synthesis, and interpretation of the lecturer's words. Engaging in it energetically and consistently will do much to ensure that you learn more from the lectures, make better grades on the tests, and acquire greater knowledge of the field.

Listen for Special Emphases. Lecturers use a variety of signals to indicate when they are saying something they consider especially important. One will raise or lower his voice. Another will say, "The thing to remember is ..." or other words that show she attaches importance to this point. One may repeat, perhaps in slightly different words, the major points and ideas. Some will pause, or speak more slowly, when covering a point of unusual importance.

Whenever a lecturer enumerates points in "one, two, three" fashion, you can be reasonably sure that these are important points. Since there are so many different ways of indicating the importance of points, no pat formula for recognizing them can be given. Identifying them is up to your own alertness and perceptiveness, but you may be sure that in most instances the cues that these are important points will be present. You need to be watching for these cues.

Taking Good Notes

Taking a good set of notes on a lecture is the surest single way of concentrating on the lecture and fixing in your mind the ideas the lecturer covers. As a bonus, good notes provide you with a remarkably simple and profitable means of reviewing what was said.

Taking notes is to the lecture what your marginal notes were to the text. Your lecture notes are literally records of the high points and most significant details of what the professor is saying. The skill that you developed in making concise marginal notes of what you read will transfer almost totally to skill in taking good notes on a lecture you are listening to, and vice versa. The biggest difference is that in taking notes on a lecture you have little time to think and consider what you are going to write. You must take notes so fast that your condensation of what you are hearing into a few words must become almost automatic. You do not have time to stop and figure out how best to express what the instructor was saying, or where this particular note should fit into the over-all scheme of the note-taking pattern you are using. You must write your notes on the run, as it were. Even this skill can be practiced quite effectively in your reading by forcing yourself to construct your marginal notes briefly and at a high rate of speed, even though circumstances would permit you to proceed in a leisurely manner, thinking them out and carefully inscribing them as slowly as you wish.

Here are several principles to learn and follow in order to take notes more effectively. Practice and perfect your skill in taking lecture notes by following these guidelines.

Record the Speaker's Ideas in Your Own Words. The necessity of listening for thoughts and ideas in addition to words and facts already has been stressed. When you make a note of a fact or idea the lecturer brings out, write it in your own words. If you can say what he has said, but put it into your own words, you probably understand the topic; you are unlikely to be merely parroting words or phrases that your ears heard. Rephrasing the lecturer's words requires a high degree of mental activity and concentration, which in itself helps you learn and remember the maximum amount from the lecture you are hearing. Obviously, having previewed the lecture by your advance study of the subject is extremely helpful here. Without already having in mind at least a sketchy idea of the whole topic, you will hardly be able to keep up with what the speaker is saying and simultaneously translate it into your own words.

There are, of course, some times when it is best to record the exact words of the instructor. Your judgment is your only resource for identifying the exceptional instance when a verbatim quotation rather than your summary statement is needed. The practice you obtain taking notes on your reading assignments, as described in Chapter 2, will help you quickly build up skill and accuracy in taking good notes on lectures.

Be Brief. Do not include such unnecessary words as *a, an,* or *the,* or prepositions and conjunctions that do not affect meaning or thought. Pick crucial nouns, verbs, and modifiers and record these as your notes. Look at the magazine advertisements of "shorthand" consisting of abrvns of wrds wch u cn rcgnz ezly & wrk up ur on s-hnd for not-takg if u wsh. (Just watch that this does not ruin your regular spelling!) Using a few symbols for commonly used, hard-to-write words can speed up your note-taking tremendously. Be sure, though, that you write all this *legibly.* Do not scribble so hurriedly that later you cannot even read your own notes.

Do not try to write down *everything* the lecturer says. This gets back to the first guide—boil down, condense, pick the concentrated grains of thought from words and write these in your notes. Leave out the embroidery. You are not to transcribe what is said, as a stenographer might do, but to translate the ideas into your own words. If you try to get down everything he or she says, you quickly will become disgusted with the whole process of taking notes and abandon it as hopeless. If you take notes discriminatingly, you can end each class period with a real addition to your knowledge of the subject.

You will find that most speakers space their important ideas throughout their lectures, elaborating with less important, explanatory material in between major points. This gives you time to get the important points into your notes without falling behind in listening.

Make Notes of Ideas, Not Merely Topic Headings. Do not mistake recording the title of a topic for getting the gist of the topic. Of course, you will not make this fatal mistake if you conscientiously work at recording the speaker's thoughts instead of his or her precise words. An outline may well consist of topic headings, but these are not adequate for classroom notes. A lecturer may be discussing types of legislatures and identify the bicameral and unicameral, with the nature and advantages and disadvantages of each. Be sure you do not leave the classroom with your notes consisting of the headings he or she talked about: "Bicameral—nature—advantages—disadvantages—Unicameral—nature—advantages—disadvantages . . .," but having omitted what the speaker said that fell under those headings.

Take As Many Notes As You Conveniently Can. Of course, you do not want to spend every minute of every class period writing so furiously that at the end of the course you do not know what the instructor looks like, but for most effective note-taking you should keep your pen or pencil fairly busy during a period. Some students fail in their note-taking attempts because they sit and wait for an earth-shattering pronouncement from the instructor before writing anything down on their paper. Most knowledge of most subjects comes in the form of gradual accumulation of significant material rather than learning an occasional fact or idea of overwhelming importance. By all means, keep your notes brief, but take notes of many things said!

The correlation between the number of notes students take in class (intelligently designed notes, that is) and their grades on the course may never have been computed, but it probably would be so high as to astound everyone—except the instructors. They know the value of good notes! So take notes steadily throughout the lecture, even though at the moment you may not see how this or that material is very relevant. When you complete the notes for the period, usually you will be able to see how important ideas emerged from the lecture, even though they may not have been clearly identifiable to you at the time. You may be surprised to find how closely you now are listening to lectures in the process of getting these good, helpful notes.

Systematize Your Notes as Soon as Possible. Probably it is best to have a loose-leaf notebook with a separate section for each of your courses. This makes it simple to keep all notes on a subject together and to add pages at appropriate places if for some reason you want to elaborate on a topic previously covered. Do not fill every line of every page with as many words as you can squeeze on it. Spread out your notes somewhat as you take them. Leave sufficient space so that as you review the notes later you can jot down additional ideas or clarifying words you remember but did not have time to get down during the class period. Do your best to indicate major points as you take your notes, by indenting, underlining, numbering and/or lettering, or any other system that you choose.

You now see that taking notes on a lecture actually is a form of recitation. You are expressing the ideas of another person in your own words, rather than merely listening to those ideas. Taking notes serves much the same purpose in listening that the **State** step serves when you read a textbook. You will recall our emphasis on how much more effective this restating is than merely re-reading pages.

Applying the PQRST procedure to listening to a lecture, this **State** step is accomplished in two stages: (1) *taking* the notes in class, which we have considered above, and (2) *reviewing* the notes after class.

Reviewing a Lecture

Just as testing yourself on pages you have studied is important in fixing material in your memory, so reviewing your notes on a lecture within twenty-four hours after taking them will aid you greatly in increasing your memory and comprehension of the ideas presented in the lecture. We already have mentioned the importance of systematizing your notes. A good time to systematize and perfect your notes of the last lecture you heard is when you sit down to study your next assignment of the subject. Systematizing and reviewing your notes, fortunately, can be done as one operation.

Run through your entire mass of notes on a lecture to see if the organization you used when taking them is adequate. See if your hurried outline form is both accurate and satisfactory to you. What are the main points? How do the various details fit under these major points? If your outline broke down somewhere along the line, now is the time to re-number it, or re-letter it, or otherwise clarify it. Some people like to identify each detail in their notes by further and further subdivisions; however, generally, identifying major points and the subpoints directly supporting them is sufficient to give your outline the system and structure needed to organize the entire lecture into a meaningful pattern.

Bear in mind that the value of systematizing your notes and reviewing them does not lie primarily in perfecting your numbering system or in routinely reading them over. The real value lies in thinking about the significance of each group of words, recalling the elaborations that the instructor presented but which you did not have time to write down, and, where appropriate, inserting such elaborations as you feel are necessary to give you a permanent, full record of the lecture.

Summarizing

Sometimes the most effective form of note-taking is summarizing. A summary is a brief statement—sometimes a sentence, sometimes a paragraph or two—which gives the essential elements of the material that was covered at greater length in the chapter or lecture. Expressed differently, it is a short statement of the crucial ideas presented by the writer or speaker, a review of the facts and concepts. This is a valuable learning aid (sometimes found in textbooks) that helps you in the **Preview** step of the PQRST study plan.

It will help you learn, review, and remember general, non-technical material which has been explained and discussed at some length if you will write a summary of it *yourself*. In dealing with highly complex and technical data, the summary is not adequate—you need notes and outlines for that sort of material. Where you have comparatively few ideas presented, however, with each idea being discussed at considerable length, you may summarize the chapter or assignment, or the lecture, by putting down the main ideas brought out with only a few words explaining each one of them.

In Chapter 2, the great value of summarizing the key ideas of paragraphs in marginal notes was discussed as an aid to performing the **State** step in your study. Making such marginal notes is an excellent way to summarize material. Making them guarantees that your mind is reacting to what you read. Your ability to summarize a paragraph in a few words written in the margin of your book indicates that you have *comprehended* what you have read or heard. You have perceived its significance and implications.

Some lectures may be more effectively reflected by summarizing than by making an outline of them. For example, an instructor might spend an entire period discussing the difference between poetry and simple verse. In doing so he or she might explain the difference in much detail, with many illustrations, but all building up one concept and not easily susceptible to an *A, B, C,* or *I, II, III* enumeration of points. Summarizing also may be most appropriate when what you want is the gist of a mass of technical words, phrases, and sentences (as in the cartoon below), whether you are hearing or reading them.

The tax levied and imposed herein upon every resident of this State, which tax shall be levied, collected, and paid annually, with respect to the net income of the taxpayer as herein defined, and upon income earned within the State of every non-resident having a business or agency in this State, computed at the following rates after deducting

---IN OTHER WORDS, IF I LIVE OR MAKE MONEY IN THIS STATE, I PAY TAXES TO IT EVERY YEAR!

Summarizing

STUDY HELPS

1. What factor in learning is inhibited by listening with your mind relaxed? List several techniques which can help you avoid this bad habit.

2. Look over some lecture notes you have taken recently. How could you improve your note-taking procedures?

3. How is taking lecture notes in your own words a form of summarizing?

Chapter 4

PSYCHOLOGICAL FACTORS INFLUENCING
LEARNING
Chapter Outline

You learn more efficiently when you:
want to learn (*Motivation*)
give your full attention (*Concentration*)
think about what you read (*Reaction*)
see the over-all picture of what you study (*Organization*)
understand the meaning of what you read (*Comprehension*),
and
review what you have studied (*Repetition*).
The PQRST method of study helps you accomplish all these
things.

We have seen that learning does not take place in any
mysterious or inexplicable manner. Neither do we learn
by automatically absorbing what we read or hear, without
putting forth mental effort. Learning is a very definite
process which takes place according to well-defined rules
and principles. In this chapter we will consider the six
factors identified in the chapter outline above which,
operating properly, promote effective information
processing and cause learning to take place efficiently.
Throughout the chapter you may note the relationship
between one or the other of these factors and concepts
developed in earlier chapters.

Motivation

Motivation means having a desire to do something.
You are said to be "motivated" when you study if you (1)
know exactly what you want to get from your study, and
(2) are really interested in getting it. A person is motivated

to do a job when he knows exactly what he is expected to do and realizes why he must do it.

If you think back for a minute, you can see how important motivation is. How much do you remember of what an instructor says in the average class you sit through? Now stop and think how much you remembered when someone was telling you how to do something you really wanted to learn to do! You remembered a great deal more when someone was telling you how to operate a new automobile you wanted to drive than when you were just sitting through a lecture in which you had no interest, didn't you? This was largely due to the fact that you were getting something you were looking for and something you wanted to get because you could see how it was going to be to your advantage to get it. In that situation you had the factors that produce good motivation.

Read For Ideas—Not To Cover Pages.

In order to be motivated in preparing a lesson, and therefore learn it better and more easily, you should do two things for every assignment you study. First, determine clearly in your own mind what you must get from this assignment or period. This is called determining the "objectives" of the assignment. The **Question** step of the PQRST method is one way to do this. Make your objective definite. Don't mumble, "I must learn something about proteins." Make yourself figure out exactly what it is you should bring away from that assignment or period that you didn't have when you went into it—perhaps in this case, what proteins are, their principal sources, and the function they serve in the human organism.

Second, answer the question, "How is this material going to help me in my future life?" Remember, material is not put into a school curriculum to fill up the college catalog or support the faculty. The answer to this question is there, so look for it. You will not be highly motivated to study a lesson unless you can determine ways that the material is going to be of use to you. Always tie in the material you are studying as closely as possible with the work you may be expected to do in your career, or needs you may encounter, and study everything with an eye to its value to you in something you may face later in life.

Poetry, novels, or essays, for example, in your literature course are not put into the college curriculum just to fill space and take your time. They can give insights into human nature and give examples of how people may react to one another or to situations. Studying literature is not merely an intellectual exercise to be engaged in for its own sake; it expands our perception of people and how their minds may work, and our grasp of how language can be used to best effect.

If all else fails, remember that you will need to know this material for exams!

Concentration

The second factor required for learning is *concentration*. By this we mean focusing your *full* attention, the *full* power of your mind, on the material you are attempting to learn. One-half of your attention is practically useless for learning. The 50 per cent of attention that you give is

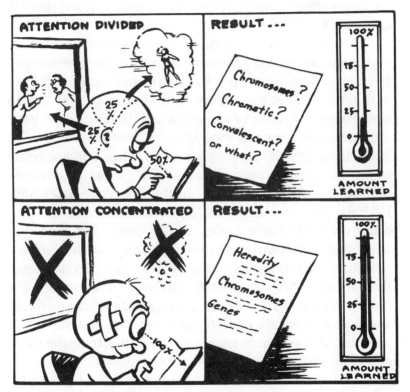

Concentration Makes The Difference!

largely wasted. When working with just 50 per cent attention, you "take in" the information presented to you, it is true, but it is the *last* 50 per cent of attention lying between "just sort of noticing" and 100 per cent attention that enables you to understand and remember the material. The first 50 per cent of attention will get the facts and ideas

from your ears or eyes to your mind, but it will not enable
your mind to *use* that material, and it will not *retain* that
material. Information and ideas stop at the "edge" of the
mind, as it were, and fade out quickly when only 50 per
cent attention is given to them. Fifty per cent attention
may not even lift what you read from the sensory intake
into your short-term memory; it certainly will not carry it
into long-term learning.

There are certain mechanical things which can assist
you in concentrating. One very simple practice: when you
study, try to have your physical surroundings so that they
will not catch your attention. It doesn't take a genius to
know which is going to win out when the contest for your
attention lies between the history of the ancient Greeks
and *His* or *Her* picture on your desk. When you are going
to study, go to a room where as few things as possible
compete with the subject matter for your attention.
Perhaps you *can* learn while you are listening to some
other students talking over in the corner, or watching
television, or looking at your new dress, or the football
schedule, or souvenirs from last night—but why do things
the hard way? Why not just get all those things out of sight
or hearing when you have to study, get the studying done,
and then sit and talk and dream about them as long as you
want to? To have more genuinely free time, take one thing
at a time, and *study* when you are *studying*!

If you get into the habit of going to a certain place at a
certain time to study, you will find that it becomes easier
for you to concentrate. You lose less time in warming up to
your subject because you will unconsciously begin to get
into the proper frame of mind for study when you come to
your study place at the study time you have selected.
When doing this becomes a habit, you have made valuable
progress because it is then easier to make yourself go
through your study routine. In other words, going to a

regular place at a regular time for study not only enables you to get started studying more easily and to study more effectively, but also substitutes the *habit of study* for will power.

A Time And Place For Study And Nothing Else Gives Best Results.

Reaction

We already have seen that learning is an active process, not just "absorbing." If you were like a sponge, and without any effort on your part could absorb knowledge as it was poured upon you, the school officials doubtless would put you in situations where you could simply sit and be educated. But this is impossible. You are not a sponge. Rather, you are more like a man out in center field who has to run, whirl, and jump to latch on to the balls batted out there! Education, in the final analysis, depends entirely upon *your taking an active part in the learning situations* in which the school puts you. When you encounter new ideas, facts, or principles, you are in a "learning situation," and as you *react* to those facts, etc., you learn as a result of *your action* in that situation. You learn only from *participating* in that situation.

Learning is directly proportionate to the amount of *reaction* you give to a learning situation, to how much you put your mind to thinking and really working on the ideas you are supposed to learn. We all know the difference between trying hard to figure out or understand something and just daydreaming about it. It is very easy, when listening to a lecture or when reading an assignment, to prop your feet up on the chair in front of you, lean your head back, relax your mind and body, and let the flow of information come from the speaker to your ears, or from the book to your eyes. Unfortunately, if your ears or eyes are the only parts of you that are active, your ears or eyes are going to be the only parts of you that take in the information. Certainly your brain will not! The information will flow to the working members, all right—the ears or eyes—but if nothing is active beyond them, it will stop right there, or pass right on through the void and out! It will never get above the sensory intake level; it will be like those dozens of faces you see on the street without noticing or remembering any of them. Information will not be taken into your brain, much less become long-term learning, unless your brain is active and is seeking to catch and use the information. *Unless your brain works on that information, you will not learn it.*

Reaction Leads To Learning.

Much of the value of the **State** step of the PQRST method lies in the fact that it requires vigorous reaction on the part of the reader. Anything you can do to guarantee definite mental action on your part when you are listening or reading will assist you in learning. Since in many cases the number of hours you sit in class is determined *for* you, it seems only sensible for you to make them count for as much as possible, so you will not have to spend additional minutes or hours outside class in order to learn material you already have heard.

One way of promoting *reaction* is taking notes in class or while reading. To restate what the speaker or author has said and put it in your own words, as you must do in order to make notes on it, you must really *think* about that material, and this is mentally *reacting*. Then you will be learning. Note-taking is one of the best devices for keeping your mind alert and busy on what your eyes or ears are taking in. Such mental reaction, remember, is absolutely essential to learning. Learning will not take place unless there is mental reaction of some sort to what is being heard or read.

A second good way to ensure mental reaction is to ask yourself at the beginning of a period (as in the **Question** step in reading), "What should I get from this discussion? Make up in your own mind some questions which you feel should be answered in the classroom discussion or lecture, or the textbook assignment, and then watch for the answers to those questions. This gives you something definite to accomplish in your listening or reading and forces your mind, as well as your eyes and ears, to be active in the process of learning.

Organization

You cannot learn a subject effectively simply by memorizing all the facts about it. Before you are able to use material you have learned, you must perceive the *organization* of that material, the way it all fits together to build up a complete picture. When an instructor starts talking, he has in his mind a general pattern of information and ideas which he wants to get across to you. Unless you recognize the general picture he is attempting to paint, you likely will be lost in the details.

Fit the Facts and Ideas into an Organized Picture.

Remember how much easier it is to fit the pieces of a jigsaw puzzle together if you have first seen the completed picture? The same idea holds true in a lecture or a chapter in your textbook. If you can get the over-all idea of what it is all about and comprehend the main points the author or teacher is trying to put across, you will be able to follow each individual idea more easily and fit in each piece of information more intelligently. If you see the big picture, you can decide much more easily and accurately where each point the teacher or author gives fits in. This procedure is known as the "whole-to-part" method. First, you get the general pattern of what you are going to learn; then you get the details in your more concentrated study. Looking over the course outline or workbook (if you have either) at the beginning of a course is an excellent way to get the general picture of what is to be accomplished in the course. Carefully studying the table of contents of the text can also give you a preview.

When you stop and think about it, the way *organization* helps convert what we study into long-term learning is simple and obvious. In the first place, a big block of knowledge can be located in your memory bank more surely and easily than can one small detail. In the second place, if you have in your mind the whole pattern of a topic, you can recall details of the topic by one detail reminding you of another, that one reminding you of still another, and so on. Furthermore, if you have a grasp of the entire scope and pattern of a topic, this will help you recall details, because you may realize that there is a gap in what you have recalled—your pattern is not complete.

You have used this procedure, just naturally and not really knowing what you were doing or that you were doing it, when you answered essay test questions. You have looked at a question and thought, "All I remember about this is . . . I'll put *that* down . . . I'm going to strike out on this one for sure." Then, as you considered how to put *that* down, you were reminded of something else that had not immediately come to your mind, and this reminded you of still something more, and finally you composed a fairly decent answer to the question that you initially drew almost a blank on. You used a rough, unconscious grasp of the *organization* of the subject material the question covered and your *comprehension* of the over-all topic to trace down details you could not have recalled as separate, unrelated items.

Think how much better you can do this in the future if you carefully study to organize material in your mind rather than having just a vague, almost accidental smattering of *organization*. Think how much it will help you on tests, and also how seeing the *organization* of material may make what you learn more meaningful to you in life generally.

Comprehension

The fifth factor in successful learning is *comprehension*. Actually, this is the real goal toward which the previous four factors are leading. *Reaction* is necessary because *comprehension* results from analyzing and synthesizing (which are reactive processes) facts and ideas. *Organization* is necessary because one must perceive the

Get The Meaning, Not Just The Words!

interrelation between principles and bits of information before their significance and meaning can be comprehended. *Motivation, reaction, organization,* and *concentration* are analogous to the four legs of a table . . . with *comprehension* as the table top. The legs are necessary because of their support of the top, but it is the *top* of the table that does that for which the table is bought and used.

Comprehension is similar in meaning to understanding. It means perceiving the significance, catching the implications, recognizing the application or reason for something, *getting the sense* of something. The child who said, "I pledge a legion to the flag of the United States of American and the Republic for Itchy Sands," obviously had learned sounds without comprehending their significance. Another classic example was the student translating Caesar's Gallic Wars who, when asked what tribe Caesar was fighting in the assignment he was translating, had not the slightest idea. And, of course, there is the typist who produces a perfect copy of a letter . . . therefore obviously having read it . . . but who has no idea what the letter was about.

Comprehension is grasping the principle involved, getting the key concept, organizing information and ideas so that they become *knowledge* instead of a hodgepodge of random facts. Obviously, this is what you, as a student, are supposed to be doing when you read an assignment or listen to a lecture.

Comprehension is the final, crowning step in converting what you study into meaningful, long-term learning. It involves grasping the pattern or organization of a topic or subject and also understanding the significance, the meaning and implications, of the subject. All this fixes the material more solidly in your memory and gives you more cues by which you can locate it, recall it, retrieve it, when you want to do so.

An excellent way of learning to identify and comprehend basic ideas and principles you encounter in your studies is to try to state the writer or teacher's thoughts in your own words, as in the **State** step. To put the material learned to best use in your own life and work, however, you must formulate its essential components into a pattern that makes sense in *your* mind (within the bounds of accuracy, of course). In this re-thinking of the whole subject you come to see more clearly the true issues, the basic ideas, the real problem under consideration.

You doubtless have had the experience of working on a problem, hunting, groping blindly in the dark for a solution. Then, suddenly, like a flash of light, you saw into the whole problem. You saw what the key point was. This is called getting "insight" into the problem. When this takes place you have *comprehended* the problem. You have a real grasp of the main, important idea. Much more often, however, comprehension or understanding is *gradually* achieved, only after perceiving, bit by bit, what all the material adds up to. In looking over your notes or in reading assigned material, do not stop when you have "gone over" it. Keep working on it until you find the main idea, the basic concept involved. When you have *comprehended* the material, you will be able to use it and you will remember it, but you will neither remember nor be able to use it well unless you understand its basic ideas.

Repetition

Few things that happen to us are so vivid that they are learned in one trial. Generally speaking, in order to remember a thing we must *repeat* it. Material studied for fifteen minutes a day for four days, or even for fifteen minutes a week for four weeks, is likely to be remembered better than material studied an hour one time and never reviewed. This procedure is known as the "principle of distributed practice." If you want to get most from the hours you spend studying, the type of repetition commonly called "review" will give you better comprehension and better memory than will study concentrated at one time, with no review.

Although repetition is essential to learning, repetition alone does not guarantee learning. You may "go over" material twenty-five times without learning it. In order for your *repetition* to do you any good, you must apply the principles of *motivation, concentration, reaction, organization,* and *comprehension*. Only as you bring all of these principles into play will your *repetition* produce long-term learning.

Repetition seldom should consist of re-reading the material. Remember, the most effective type of review is not re-reading material but mentally working to force yourself to *recall* the material read, referring to the textbook or your notes only to get the sequence of the material and to check and supplement your memory. This is hard work, but results in much better learning and memory than does mere re-reading.

The repetition called *review* is particularly helpful in depositing material studied in your storehouse of long-term learning. Here is the reason: Forgetting takes place most rapidly shortly after you stop studying a subject. The greatest loss is within a few hours. The speed with which you forget gradually slows down as time goes on. If possible, arrange your study so as to review material about twelve to twenty-four hours after it is first studied, a second time about a week after that, and finally about three weeks later. You will find that this distribution of practice is a review schedule which will be helpful in ensuring the maximum memory of material you have studied. Perhaps you will not have time to review all your study material at these specified intervals and in detail, but you should carefully select the material that it is *especially important* for you to remember and review it according to this schedule.

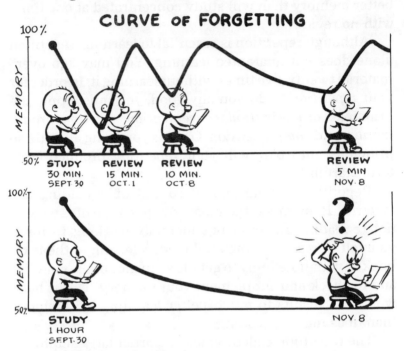

To Understand The Function And Importance Of Review,
You Should Understand The Curve Of Forgetting.

Remember, you *do not*, repeat, you *do not* become an efficient learner by reading these principles of learning. Good long-term learning comes only through practicing them until you become skillful in using them and then habitually using them in your studying.

As you see, the PQRST system of study promotes the action of each of these psychological factors contributing to learning. But they will help you even more if you consciously and deliberately think of them and try to bring them to bear on your studying.

STUDY HELPS

1. Good *motivation* requires:

   (1)

   (2)

2. What effect does raising your degree of *concentration* from 50 to 100 per cent have on the amount you learn?

3. You can encourage your brain to *react* to a lecture by:

   (1)

   (2)

4. What step of the PQRST system helps you use the whole-to-part approach to a topic you are studying? How?

5. List at least six synonyms for or expressions illustrating what is involved in *comprehension*.

6. How are the "principle of distributed practice" and the "curve of forgetting" related?

Chapter 5

CLASS DISCUSSION

Chapter Outline

"Intake" and "Output" as learning experiences
Types of classroom questions
Inappropriate and appropriate participation in discussion
Preparing to participate in class discussions

Up to this point, this book has been devoted to discussing principles of learning you can capitalize on in gaining long-term memory of subject matter assigned in your courses, and has presented an effective, efficient method of studying that will aid you in getting the most learning from the time you spend studying. Often you will be trying to achieve this long-term learning through study in the form of reading assignments. Other times you will be adding to your knowledge and understanding of the subject through listening to lectures. We have seen how following the PQRST method of studying can assist you in both of these avenues of learning. We might call studying through reading or listening the "intake" part of your education.

Just as there are principles of learning and methods of studying that add to the effectiveness of your "intake," there are some guides you may follow that will increase the effectiveness of the "output" part, for, as every student knows, there are times when the instructor requires evidence of your having developed the knowledge and understandings he deems necessary for students in that particular course. Then you need to be able to show that you indeed have achieved the learning outcomes he expects. Usually the two ways in which you will have opportunity to demonstrate your mastery of the material will be through participating in class discussions and through the test or examination papers you write.

Obviously, not all teachers follow the same procedures. Some like for members of their classes to talk about the topics under consideration, and to express their ideas. Some do not. Some call on students by name to answer specific questions posed, or to discuss specific topics. Others ask questions of the class at large. Each has reasons for his or her procedures, and you will benefit more from the course if you cooperate with the method employed. If it is evident that he or she invites discussion, or asks questions either to individuals or the class at large, it will be advantageous to you to prepare yourself to participate appropriately.

Answering questions may require reasoning as well as recall of facts. "What were some of the social and economic effects of the New Deal?" is a question which probably could be answered on the basis of recall of facts gained from reading the textbook. "What would be the difference in the reception an economic innovation such as the New Deal would receive today and the reception it received in the thirties, and what would account for that difference?" would require thoughtful analysis and synthesis of the extensive array of facts you possess. By carrying out the **Question** and **State** steps of the PQRST method of studying, you can anticipate and prepare to answer all types of questions that might be asked in class.

Sometimes a teacher will open the door to general discussion by asking something like, "What topics in today's assignment would you like to explore further than our author takes us?" or "What ideas in this chapter did you find most provocative of thought?" Here he or she is inviting the interests of the class to direct the discussion, and imaginative use of the **Question** step in studying will have given you the background to take advantage of this opportunity. An instructor will evaluate your mental alertness and capacity for discriminating thought by the degree to which your imagination and curiosity have carried you beyond merely remembering what the author wrote.

Whenever a teacher invites questions, comments, or discussion, you are being given an opportunity to demonstrate your knowledge and understanding of the topic at hand. In evaluating you, a teacher will take into consideration your willingness and ability to respond appropriately to such opportunities. Some do this by giving a specific grade each time a student answers a question. Some do it by forming a mental evaluation of the general quality of the student's oral participation and considering this when making out final grades. In either case, it will be to your advantage to have participated knowledgeably in class discussions.

There is a happy medium to strive for in gauging the extent of your participation in class discussions. On one undesirable extreme is the person who never accepts any responsibility for contributing to the class and who sits mute unless specifically called upon. At the other undesirable extreme is the student who always has something (or *much!*) to say on everything. Because of his lower inhibitions about speaking out, being faster in his mental processes, or being more knowledgeable on the subject, he tends to monopolize any discussion, crowding out willing but less aggressive participants. In between is the student all teachers using discussion as a medium of instruction like to have in their classes. This is the person who is always willing and able to contribute his part to the discussion, but who limits his participation to an amount that encourages others to speak, too. Hitting this happy medium is not a difficult or impossible thing. The typical college student has developed a pretty good sense of social appropriateness, and if he will apply this to the question, "How much should I talk in class?" he usually will have an amply sufficient guide.

Talking Too Much Or Too Little In Class Is Equally Bad.

What to say is a greater problem than *how much* to say or *how frequently* to speak. You may not be very experienced in talking about your ideas and thoughts on subjects such as English literature or psychology, but here the PQRST system again helps you. In the **Question** step, as you studied the assignment, you formulated questions to guide you. Either an unanswered question or one that extends a topic beyond the area covered in the text is legitimate and proper to ask if given the opportunity in class.

Does the instructor ask for discussion of some topic? In carrying out the **State** step as you studied, you practiced expressing the ideas of the text in your own words. In both the **Question** and **State** steps you used your imagination and initiative to develop proficiency in thinking and talking about the topic under consideration, and this proficiency will transfer to increase your ability to talk intelligently on topics on which the instructor invites discussion.

It is as simple as this: If you have practiced asking yourself questions about a topic and expressing your thoughts about it, you will be able to discuss that topic better when a teacher gives you an opportunity to do so. You will be able to speak more coherently and to demonstrate your knowledge, understanding, and reasoning power to better advantage.

Bear this in mind: When an instructor asks for questions or comments, he *wants* questions or comments. Students who give them are fulfilling part of his expectations of them. He properly takes this into consideration in determining the over-all performance of students in the course.

. . . and remember classroom courtesy!

STUDY HELPS

1. How can a student gauge the appropriate amount of participation in discussions?

2. In what way does the **Question** step in studying prepare one for appropriate class participation?

3. What benefit may one derive from having gone through the **State** step as he prepared for a class meeting?

Chapter 6

EXAMS!

Chapter Outline

Preparing for an examination
Taking objective tests
Taking essay tests

There is all the difference in the world between reviewing and cramming. Cramming is a frantic attempt to stuff one's mind as full as possible of facts and ideas in and for a short time. Review is a re-examination of familiar material to clarify one's understanding, refresh one's memory, and pick up any important material which has been overlooked or has slipped out of mind. The crammer reads, reads, reads, trying doggedly and desperately to cover in a night everything he should have learned in a term. Typically he tries to semi-memorize facts and concepts which

Review For Examinations, Don't Cram!

underlinings or hazy memories lead him to fear are important. Like an inept swimmer threshing wildly in the water,
he reads furiously, trying to atone by violence of concentration for his lack of comprehension.

This is not the case when you *review* material you
already have studied by the PQRST method. When you
begin to review for a test, glance at your notes on a topic, or
at the topic heading in your book, or your underlining, and
then stop and *think!* Force yourself to reconstruct the
details from memory. Make yourself restate in your own
words the main points, and elaborate on them to be sure
that you know enough about the topic. After you have
done your best to re-think it, scan the topic in the book, or
look over your notes again, to see if you overlooked anything important. (This is important. Sometimes you may
think you know a topic thoroughly when you really do
not. By scanning material as you review, you not only
know that you know it, you also refresh your memory of
it.)

If testing reveals that you did overlook something important as you mentally restated the paragraph or topic,
make a mental note to be sure to include that item in
future consideration of the topic. If you find that you
adequately covered the topic as you stated it in your own
words, determine the answer to this question, "How does
this fit into the over-all subject?" Then proceed to the next
paragraph or topic. The result? After two—or ten—hours
of study, you have systematically reconsidered the material of your course and strengthened any weak spots, as
well as gained a new appreciation of the organization of
the subject.

If you have studied assignments for a month, a quarter,
or a semester by the PQRST system, and have taken notes
and soon reviewed them as recommended, tests and examinations should not be major obstacles to you. A

reasonable amount of review, re-covering your text and notes using the **Test** step, should prepare you to do better on examinations than you have in the past. There also are a few techniques of taking tests that usually can be counted on to earn you a few extra points.

Objective Tests

If you are taking an objective test (multiple-choice, true-false, or comparable type), you probably will achieve best results by following this procedure:

(1) Read an item through quickly, with high concentration, and *answer on the basis of your first impression.*

(2) Then re-read the item, asking yourself what it really means, expressing its thought in your own words (as you did in the **State** step of PQRST and in striving for *comprehension*).

Answer An Objective-Type Question By Your First Impression, Then Analyze It Carefully To Check The Accuracy Of Your Answer.

(3) Ask yourself if your original answer still appears correct in light of your close analysis of the item, but *do not change your answer because of a mere doubt. Change it only if you find clear indication that it is wrong and another right.*

(4) Always keep in mind that your instructor is not attempting to trick you in the questions. They are designed to measure your knowledge of a subject, not your ingenuity in solving verbal puzzles. So *don't out-smart yourself* looking for devious, tricky interpretations and ignoring the obvious, straightforward meaning.

Essay Tests

In taking a test where you are to write answers in your own words, observe these guidelines:

(1) *Read the question carefully.* Then re-read it and express its meaning in your own words. Check each word in the question to be sure that your interpretation omitted nothing important. To give a satisfactory answer to a question, you have to correctly understand what it is asking.

(2) *Answer the questions you know first.* This way you will be sure not to use all your time puzzling over questions you do *not* know the answers to, and then run short of time for writing answers you know well. (You should start each answer on a separate page so that you can keep them in their proper order.)

(3) *Outline your answer* on a piece of scratch paper before starting to write it in full. In this way you can organize your thoughts and check your answer against the question for possible omissions. Writing from your outline, you can present what you know more clearly and completely than you could if you just started writing down your thoughts as they came to you.

(4) *Write with a good pen,* or a well-sharpened No. 2 pencil, so that your writing can be easily read.

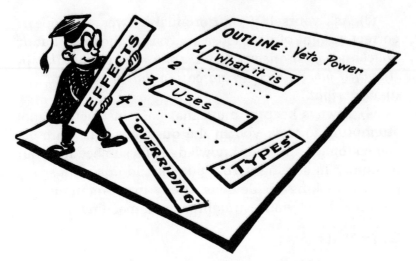

Outline Your Answer Before Writing It.

(5) *Watch your penmanship, spelling, and punctuation.* No matter how much psychology or history, or whatever, you may know, it will impress your instructor less if you answer in a near-illegible scrawl that he can hardly decipher, with your *m*'s looking like *w*'s, and your *r*'s like *n*'s, or with ornate flourishes that all but obscure the letters. As a scholar who loves his field, he is displeased if you discuss it with the misspellings of a semi-literate, or if you leave your meaning difficult or impossible to fathom because of poor punctuation.

(6) *Read over your answers* after you have finished your paper, checking for thought and completeness, as well as for spelling, punctuation, and sentence structure. All these factors are related to your mastery of course material. (How do you spell words correctly without access to a dictionary, which you are unlikely to have during tests? By noting the spelling of words that are not thoroughly familiar to you while you are studying, and looking up the spelling when you use them in papers you prepare outside of class!)

What is involved in answering a question "completely" is determined by the question wording itself and the preferences of individual professors. From the number of questions on the test and the amount of time you are allotted, yqu can form a rough approximation of how fully you should answer the questions.

(7) *Count your questions and answers* before you hand your paper in, to be sure you did not overlook any. Be sure your pages are in correct order so the instructor will not have to shuffle through them trying to sort them out.

STUDY HELPS

1. What advantage comes from forcing your mind to recall what was in a topic as you review for tests, rather than re-reading the material?

2. How should you proceed to answer questions on an objective test?

3. In what ways may you improve your examination paper by reading over answers to essay questions before handing the paper in?